0.5

First Ladies

Abigail Adams

Jill C. Wheeler

ABDO
Publishing Company

visit us at
www.abdopublishing.com

Published by ABDO Publishing Company, 8000 West 78th Street, Edina, Minnesota 55439.
Copyright © 2010 by Abdo Consulting Group, Inc. International copyrights reserved in all
countries. No part of this book may be reproduced in any form without written permission from the
publisher. The Checkerboard Library™ is a trademark and logo of ABDO Publishing Company.

Printed in the United States.

 Manufactured with paper containing at least 10% post-consumer waste

Cover Photo: Getty Images
Interior Photos: Abigail Adams Historical Society, Inc. p. 7; Alamy pp. 11, 26; Corbis pp. 11, 23;
    Getty Images p. 9; The Granger Collection p. 5; Courtesy of the Massachusetts Historical
    Society pp. 18, 21; National Park Service, Adams National Historical Park pp. 13, 16, 17, 22,
    24; North Wind pp. 15, 19, 20, 27; The White House Historical Association p. 25

Series Coordinator: BreAnn Rumsch
Editors: Heidi M.D. Elston, BreAnn Rumsch
Art Direction & Cover Design: Neil Klinepier

Library of Congress Cataloging-in-Publication Data

Wheeler, Jill C., 1964-
 Abigail Adams / Jill C. Wheeler.
    p. cm. -- (First ladies)
 Includes index.
 ISBN 978-1-60453-629-4
 1. Adams, Abigail, 1744-1818--Juvenile literature. 2. Presidents' spouses--United States--
Biography--Juvenile literature. I. Title.

 E322.1.A38W47 2010
 973.4'4092--dc22
 [B]
                              2009008178

Contents

Abigail Adams

Abigail Adams was First Lady when the United States of America was a new country. She was the wife of John Adams, the second U.S. president. She was also the mother of the sixth U.S. president, John Quincy Adams.

Mrs. Adams was one of the most **influential** women of her time. Her role in American history began before the United States was even a country. She supported the fight for independence from Great Britain.

At the time, women did not usually speak out about politics. But Mrs. Adams was different. She was not afraid to voice her beliefs. Mrs. Adams supported educating women. She also spoke out against slavery. Her opinions were not popular then. But her husband greatly valued her advice.

As a woman of the 1700s, Mrs. Adams witnessed much in her life. Throughout her years, she wrote hundreds of letters. Today, her letters provide a treasured record of that time in American history. Mrs. Adams's independent mind made her a role model for future First Ladies.

Abigail Adams's independent spirit led her to believe in an independent nation.

Early Years

Abigail Smith was born on November 22, 1744, in Weymouth, Massachusetts. Weymouth was a small, rural town. There, Abigail grew up near the coast of the Atlantic Ocean and Boston, Massachusetts.

Abigail's father was William Smith. He served as the minister in Weymouth. Abigail's mother, Elizabeth Quincy Smith, cared for the Smith household. Elizabeth came from a prominent family. The Quincys were well-known in politics.

Abigail was the second of four children. Mary was the oldest. Abigail also had a younger brother named William and a younger sister named Elizabeth.

The Smith family had a good life. They had a comfortable home and a servant to help with daily chores. Still, Elizabeth taught her daughters how to run a house. Abigail learned how to cook, clean, sew, and knit early on.

Abigail's childhood home

Love of Learning

Many of Abigail's childhood experiences shaped the adult she later became. Growing up, she was exposed to many ideas, opinions, and people. Abigail often stayed with relatives who were leaders in politics, government, and business. She learned much from listening to their conversations. She also learned much from her parents.

Elizabeth, Abigail's mother, was active in the Weymouth community. She visited the sick and took food and clothing to the poor. Abigail often joined her mother on these visits. She learned firsthand the importance of helping those who were less fortunate.

Abigail received no formal schooling. Instead, she was taught at home. She learned reading, writing, and mathematics. Abigail also studied music, dance, and Irish. But that was not enough for her.

In many ways, Abigail was like her father. William was a well-educated man who loved to read and learn. He encouraged his children to explore his large library of books. Abigail did just that. She was often seen with an open book in her hands.

Abigail became one of the most well-read women of her time. She read books about history, religion, government, and law. She also enjoyed poetry, Greek myths, and William Shakespeare's plays. Abigail even taught herself French.

Abigail was a bright girl. From a young age, she did not hesitate to express her views.

Wedding Bells

When Abigail was 15 years old, she met a lawyer named John Adams. He had graduated from Harvard College in Cambridge, Massachusetts. John was not interested in Abigail at first.

Then about two years later, John and Abigail were reintroduced. They realized they had much in common. Both were well-read and had sharp minds. By 1762, the two were exchanging many

Lifelong Partners

From 1762 to 1801, John and Abigail Adams exchanged more than 1,000 letters. The earliest letters were written during their courtship. Writing kept them close when work kept them apart.

Forty years of letters leave an important record of the times. Mr. Adams was often away serving the country. Mrs. Adams updated him about the farm and their family. She also shared news of the American Revolution.

Their letters also reveal the couple's loving relationship. Many of Mrs. Adams's letters to her husband begin with "Dearest Friend." No matter how trying their lives were, they continued to support each other.

letters. They enjoyed sharing their thoughts and feelings with each other.

At first, Abigail's parents objected to her relationship with John. He was a farmer's son. The Smiths had hoped Abigail would marry a more prominent man. They also worried Abigail was too young to marry.

Eventually, the Smiths accepted John and Abigail's love. After a long courtship, the two married on October 25, 1764. Abigail's father performed the ceremony at his church in Weymouth.

Abigail married John just a few weeks before her twentieth birthday.

Wife and Mother

The **newlyweds** made their home in Braintree, Massachusetts. This town was later renamed Quincy. There, Mr. Adams had inherited land from his father. His farm included thirty acres (12 ha) of pastures, orchards, and woods. Mr. and Mrs. Adams moved into the house next door to his childhood home.

Mrs. Adams quickly settled into her new role as a wife. She did many of the household and farm chores. She cleaned, cooked, and tended the garden. She also fed their horses, cows, sheep, and chickens.

Soon, the Adamses started a family. They had their first child on July 14, 1765. Her name was Abigail, but they called her Nabby. John Quincy arrived two years later on July 11, 1767.

On December 28, 1768, Susanna was born. Sadly, she died on February 4, 1770. Charles arrived that year on May 29. Thomas followed on September 15, 1772. In July 1777, another daughter was born. Yet, she did not survive.

Meanwhile, Mr. Adams was busy building his legal practice. He was often on the road, traveling to Boston and surrounding areas. Sometimes, he was gone for weeks or even months at a time. Mrs. Adams stayed on the farm and ran her busy household.

Mr. Adams's childhood home (right) *in Quincy is one of the oldest remaining presidential birthplaces. Another is Mr. and Mrs. Adams's first home* (left), *where John Quincy Adams was born.*

Trouble in Boston

While they were apart, Mr. and Mrs. Adams continued writing letters to each other. This kept their relationship strong. They relied on each other for advice, support, and love. Although they were miles apart, Mr. and Mrs. Adams shared their doubts and fears. They also discussed political news, including the growing tension in the colonies.

By the 1760s, the United States had not yet been formed. At the time, Massachusetts was one of 13 British colonies in North America. For several years, Great Britain had been imposing new taxes on the colonies. This angered many colonists, including Mr. and Mrs. Adams. They wanted independence from Great Britain.

In 1768, Mr. Adams was practicing law in Boston. Mrs. Adams moved their family there to be with him. Soon, Boston became the scene of several conflicts.

On March 5, 1770, a fight broke out between colonists and British soldiers. The soldiers killed five colonists. This event became known as the Boston Massacre. Then on December 16, 1773, about 60 colonists staged the Boston Tea Party. They dumped 342 chests of tea into Boston Harbor to oppose a tea tax.

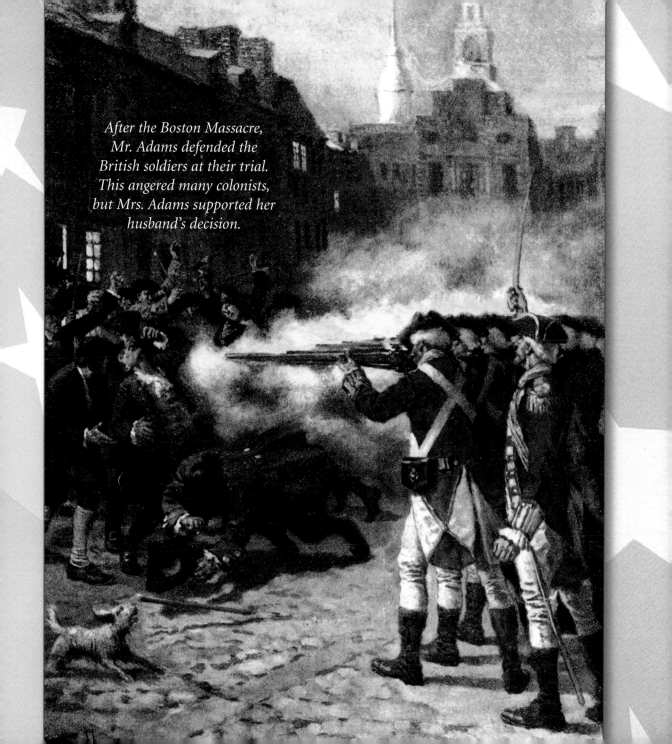

After the Boston Massacre, Mr. Adams defended the British soldiers at their trial. This angered many colonists, but Mrs. Adams supported her husband's decision.

On Her Own

In 1774, the British government passed several laws that increased British control in Massachusetts. These laws angered the colonists, so they became known as the Intolerable Acts.

The colonies decided it was time to unite. That September, the colonies sent delegates to the First **Continental Congress** in Philadelphia, Pennsylvania. Mr. Adams went as a Massachusetts representative. The Congress sought fair treatment from Great Britain.

Meanwhile, Mrs. Adams moved their children back to Braintree. There, she ran the farm and managed the family's business affairs. This was unusual at

John Quincy Adams

the time. Men usually handled financial and business matters, while women ran the household.

Yet, Mr. Adams trusted his wife to do a good job. She hired workers and oversaw planting and harvesting. She ordered supplies, bought livestock, and even purchased land.

Mrs. Adams also raised the children largely by herself. She taught them to be honest, helpful, and responsible. In addition, Mrs. Adams oversaw their education. She taught the children all she knew. She even made sure they learned French and Latin.

Nabby Adams

Revolution!

By 1775, more and more colonists were protesting British control. The **American Revolution** officially began in April. That May, Mr. Adams returned to Philadelphia to attend the Second **Continental Congress**.

Meanwhile, the war quickly became a reality for Mrs. Adams and the children. Several early battles took place in Massachusetts. Mrs. Adams knew these events were important to the future of the country. In June, the Battle of Bunker Hill occurred. Mrs. Adams took her son John Quincy to the top of nearby Penn's Hill. There, they witnessed the battle unfold.

On June 18, Mrs. Adams informed her husband about the Battle of Bunker Hill.

The Battle of Bunker Hill was the first major battle of the American Revolution. The British suffered heavy losses. This gave the colonists hope they could win the war.

Without her husband, Mrs. Adams endured many difficulties due to the war. She faced limited supplies and higher costs. Mrs. Adams struggled to support her family. Still, she kept the children fed and the farm running.

Mrs. Adams had many responsibilities at home. Yet, she never stopped writing to her husband. While he was working in Philadelphia, their letters discussed the war. Throughout these hard times, Mrs. Adams never hesitated to express her support for independence.

Fighting for Liberty

British soldiers sometimes attacked towns.
This forced colonists to leave their homes.

Mrs. Adams and her children did their part to help the fight for independence. They provided colonial soldiers with food and lodging as they marched through town. They made bullets, and they helped people fleeing from Boston.

Yet, other colonists remained loyal to England's King George III. These people were called Loyalists. During the war, Mrs. Adams questioned women suspected of being Loyalists. In this way, she helped the colonies fight the war!

At the time, Mr. Adams was still away from home. He was working with the Second **Continental Congress** to form an independent nation.

Mrs. Adams supported her husband's work. She hoped the new government would be fair to women. In March 1776, Mrs. Adams wrote her husband a letter. She encouraged him to consider women and their rights when creating new laws. She wrote, "I desire you would Remember the Ladies." This letter made Mrs. Adams one of the earliest supporters of women's rights in America.

Mrs. Adams's most famous letter to her husband

That year on July 4, Congress approved the Declaration of Independence. The document did not guarantee the rights of women. But it did declare the colonies free of British control. The United States of America was born.

Living Abroad

In 1778, Congress appointed Mr. Adams minister to France. He took John Quincy and Charles with him. Mrs. Adams was sad to see them leave. While they were gone, she rarely received news from them. It took many weeks for letters to cross the Atlantic Ocean.

The **American Revolution** ended in September 1783. The United States won its independence! Now, Mrs. Adams wanted to be with her husband. So in 1784, she and Nabby journeyed to Europe. At last, Mr. and Mrs. Adams were reunited.

Mr. Adams still had much work to do in Europe. So, they spent the next four years in France and England. Mrs. Adams hosted gatherings and offered her husband advice.

Before departing for Europe, Mr. Adams gave his wife a locket. It says, "I yield whatever is, is right."

In 1788, the Adams family returned home. The next year, the United States held its first presidential election. Mr. Adams was elected the country's first vice president. He took office on April 30, 1789, under President George Washington.

Mrs. Adams was now the first vice president's wife. She soon became friends with the First Lady, Martha Washington.

As First Lady, Mrs. Washington (above) *counted on Mrs. Adams's help. So during social occasions, she always seated Mrs. Adams to her right.*

Mrs. Adams used her experience from living in Europe to help the Washingtons entertain important guests. She spent the next eight years in this role. Then in 1796, Mr. Adams was elected president.

First Lady

On March 4, 1797, Mr. Adams took office as the second U.S. president. Mrs. Adams was now the First Lady. She received visitors each day. Sometimes, there were as many as 60! She also entertained important guests and attended public ceremonies. Once a week, Mrs. Adams hosted a dinner for congressmen and diplomats.

President Adams valued the First Lady's advice. He discussed many important matters with her. Mrs. Adams continued to support women's rights. She believed in equal education for girls and boys. She argued that educated mothers raise educated children. Mrs. Adams also supported freedom for slaves.

Mrs. Adams was not in Philadelphia to see her husband take office. She began acting as First Lady when she arrived there in May.

When Mr. Adams first became president, the U.S. capital had
been located in Philadelphia. But in 1800, it moved to Washington,
D.C. Many new buildings were being constructed there. The plans
included a home for the president, known today as the White House.

That November, Mr. and Mrs. Adams became the first family to
live in the White House. The house was not yet finished. It was
damp and cold. Still, Mrs. Adams did her best to make do.

The First Lady used the unfinished East Room to hang laundry to dry!

Last Years

Peacefield

In late 1800, Mr. and Mrs. Adams faced difficult times. Their son Charles became ill and died in December. And, President Adams lost his bid for reelection. So in March 1801, Mr. and Mrs. Adams retired to Massachusetts. Years earlier, they had purchased a home called Peacefield. They quickly settled into a quiet life there.

Mrs. Adams was content to enjoy life in the country. She entertained friends and spent time with family. She also advised and supported her son John Quincy during his political career. He served as a U.S. senator, minister to Russia, and **secretary of state**. He later became the sixth U.S. president in 1825.

Sadly, Mr. and Mrs. Adams learned their daughter Nabby had **cancer**. Mrs. Adams cared for her, but Nabby died in 1814.

When Mr. Adams died in 1826, he was buried beside his wife.

Then in 1818, Mrs. Adams became ill with **typhoid fever**. She died on October 28. She was buried at the United First Parish Church in Quincy.

Abigail Adams left her mark on American history. She was the first woman to be wife to one president and mother to another. Equally important, she was a thoughtful writer. Mrs. Adams left her **legacy** in the letters she wrote. She is remembered as a courageous patriot and a strong First Lady.

Timeline

1744	On November 22, Abigail Smith was born.
1764	On October 25, Abigail married John Adams.
1765	The Adamses' daughter Abigail, or Nabby, was born on July 14.
1767	On July 11, the Adamses' son John Quincy was born.
1768	The Adamses' daughter Susanna was born on December 28.
1770	Susanna died on February 4; the Adamses' son Charles was born on May 29.
1772	On September 15, the Adamses' son Thomas was born.
1777	In July, the Adamses' last child was born but did not survive.
1784–1788	Mrs. Adams lived in Europe during Mr. Adams's time as minister there.
1789–1797	Mr. Adams served as George Washington's vice president.
1797–1801	Mrs. Adams acted as First Lady, while her husband served as president.
1800	The U.S. capital moved to Washington, D.C.; the Adamses became the first to live in the White House; Charles died in December.
1814	Nabby died from cancer.
1818	On October 28, Mrs. Adams died.

Did You Know?

When Abigail Adams was born, Great Britain's colonies in North America used the Julian calendar. On that calendar, Mrs. Adams's birthday was November 11. Great Britain and its colonies adopted the Gregorian calendar in 1752. Then, November 11 became November 22.

Mrs. Adams stood 5 feet 1 inch (1.5 m) tall. She had brown hair and brown eyes.

Barbara Bush is the only other woman to be the wife of one president and the mother of another.

The Abigail Adams Historical Society has preserved Mrs. Adams's childhood home. It is still located in Weymouth, Massachusetts. Tourists can also visit the homes where she raised her own family. The Adams National Historical Park is located in Quincy, Massachusetts.

Mr. and Mrs. Adams are buried beside their son John Quincy and his wife, Louisa Adams.

Mrs. Adams is the first of three First Ladies buried on the grounds of a house of faith. The other two are Louisa Adams and Edith Wilson. Mrs. Wilson is buried at the Washington National Cathedral in Washington, D.C.

Glossary

American Revolution - from 1775 to 1783. A war for independence between Great Britain and its North American colonies. The colonists won and created the United States of America.

cancer - any of a group of often deadly diseases marked by an abnormal growth of cells that destroys healthy tissues and organs.

Continental Congress - the body of representatives that spoke for and acted on behalf of the 13 colonies.

influential (ihn-floo-EHN-shuhl) - having the power or ability to produce an effect on others.

legacy - something important or meaningful handed down from previous generations or from the past.

newlywed - a person who just married.

secretary of state - a member of the president's cabinet who handles relations with other countries.

typhoid fever (TEYE-foyd FEE-vuhr) - a disease that causes fever, headache, and swelling and pain of the intestine.

Web Sites

To learn more about Abigail Adams, visit ABDO Publishing Company on the World Wide Web at **www.abdopublishing.com**. Web sites about Abigail Adams are featured on our Book Links page. These links are routinely monitored and updated to provide the most current information available.

Index